BE SO CERTAIN,
THE UNIVERSE CAN'T
IGNORE *you*

This book belongs to:

Shifting Contents

Write your favorite affirmations here

Write your favorite subliminals, music or scents used for Shifting

As you trial different methods, write down what you liked or did not like about them as well as any tips for the future

Some helpful tips for before and after you shift

Make sure to include as much detail as possible!

Journal about your experiences because you are going to want to remember them!

Affirmations

I
Will
Shift

I Will
Wake Up
In My DR

Shifting
Is
Easy

Shifting Essentials

Subliminals

Music

Scents

Shifting Methods

Shifting Methods

Pre Shifting Tips

Safe Words

_____

_____

Hydrate

Meditate

Post Shifting Tips

Grounding Techniques

_____

_____

Deep Breathing

Stretch

My Script

MY SCRIPT
About Me: (Name, Nicknames, Age, Birthday, Birth Place, Gender, etc)

About Me: Physical Characteristics (Height, Weight, Hair Color/length, Hair Texture, Eye Color, Boob Size, Tattoos/Piercings, etc)

About Me: Personality Traits (Funny, Nice, Sexy, Smart, Positive Traits, Negative Traits, etc)

About Me: Anything I Don't Want (Acne, Period, Body Odor, Etc)

About Me: Favorites (Color, Animal, Book, Movie, Show, Food, Drink, Etc)

About Me: All The Details (Hobbies, Interests, Talents, Opinions, Strengths, Weaknesses, Etc)

My Relationships (Best Friends, Boyfriend/Girlfriend, Parents, Siblings, Etc)

Time In My DR (i.e. 1 hour in my CR = 1 day in my DR)

Where I Will Live In My DR

Other Important Rules In My DR: (No death, No homophobia, Clones, Etc)

My Script (in detail)

My Shifting Experiences

103

Made in the USA
Las Vegas, NV
04 September 2021